or before

floral   inspirations

Published in the UK by British Teleflower Service Ltd.   ISBN 0 9536565 0 0

contents

floral

Flowers are a popular and enduring feature of both home and office life. They lend warmth, colour and light to any environment and make a gift that is welcome worldwide.

This book is a celebration of
floral design. It touches on the
principles and elements of
design technique - and offers a
glimpse into the creative ideas
that bring them to life.

inspirations

However simple or complex an
arrangement, its effectiveness will
usually be based on these
fundamental principles of design:–

- good balance and proportion

- striking contrasts

- a pleasing harmony and scale

- a strong dominant theme

- rhythm - the ability to draw

  the eye effortlessly from one

  element of a design to another

That said, good design is as much about instinct as it is about technique. The secret

lies in how you use the elements of the design - the colour and texture of materials,

the form of the arrangement and the space around it - to bring those principles to life.

9

This book is a unique
showcase of arrangements
created by some of the
country's leading floral
designers - world champions
and Chelsea gold medal
winners among them.

Some of the designs are intricate; others breathtakingly bold and simple. Some obey all the rules; some don't.

All of them share the one ingredient that transforms a competent design into a work of art.

Imagination.

the
principles

Good design makes imaginative use of the colour, size and type of materials to achieve both

bala

contrast

and dimension to a design, and draws the eye to key points of interest.

However, it is also important that the elements should combine

well to lend unity and consistency to the overall appearan

17

Colour, form,

texture, line and

movement - all

work together to

deliver the

design's effect

18

19

dominance

Allow a single line, colour, shape or texture to control the design. This gives it clarity and focus and makes it easier for the eye to appreciate.

scale &

Good design establishes a pleasing size relationship between the components of an arrangement.

That may mean applying traditional rules (such as two-thirds flower to one-third container).

Or it may not.

proportion

Deciding what makes an arrangement the right size is

ultimately a question of judgement and confidence.

What matters is that the

physical size and quantity of

flowers is suited to the context

they appear in - whether a vase,

a base or a bride's bouquet.

movement

When the rhythm of a piece is right, the eye is drawn naturally from one area of interest to another. This is often achieved by echoing themes of colour and shape (in varying sizes) throughout the design.

TO28904

the elements

colour

Probably the most important

element of any design is its

use of colour - whether based

on a single hue, or a variety of

colours that either complement

or contrast with one another.

The sheer variety of flower types and colours

available to the modern designer can sometimes be

overwhelming - learning how to pick and combine

colours to best effect is a skill in itself.

The secret lies in stimulating the eye, without tiring it.

form

Also important is the

form - or outline -

created by the

arrangement of the

design's physical

components. This

acts as a template -

determining where

the areas of interest

must lie to achieve

best visual impact.

s p a c e

Good design is as much

about what you leave out

as about what you put in.

Creative use of space gives

the eye breathing room -

accentuating key features.

texture

The texture of a design is defined in terms of both its actual, physical texture and its visual textural appearance. Varying textures (of flowers, containers and props) can often be combined effectively to create a design with genuine contrast and interest.

imagination

The most important
ingredient of all: the
ability to stretch
yourself, using everyday
materials in an everyday
context, to produce a
design that is striking
and unique.

It might be the

centrepiece for a living

room coffee table.

Or an eye-catching

window-display to

highlight a promotion.

40

41

Unleashing your
imagination gives an
extra dimension to
your floral designs.

The results are

sometimes spectacular,

occasionally bizarre –

and always interesting.

42

43

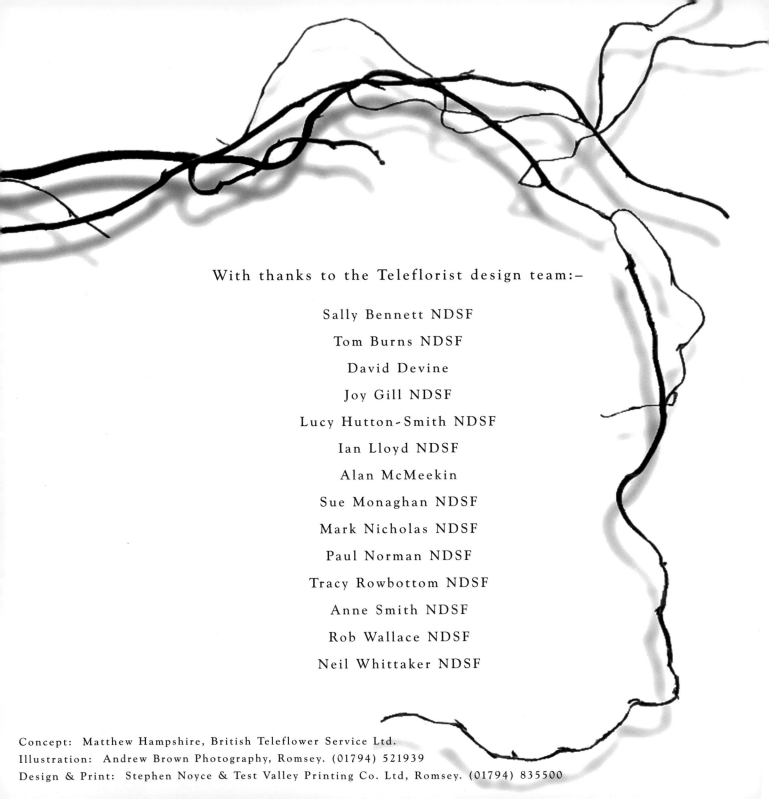

With thanks to the Teleflorist design team:–

Sally Bennett NDSF

Tom Burns NDSF

David Devine

Joy Gill NDSF

Lucy Hutton-Smith NDSF

Ian Lloyd NDSF

Alan McMeekin

Sue Monaghan NDSF

Mark Nicholas NDSF

Paul Norman NDSF

Tracy Rowbottom NDSF

Anne Smith NDSF

Rob Wallace NDSF

Neil Whittaker NDSF

Concept: Matthew Hampshire, British Teleflower Service Ltd.
Illustration: Andrew Brown Photography, Romsey. (01794) 521939
Design & Print: Stephen Noyce & Test Valley Printing Co. Ltd, Romsey. (01794) 835500

TELEFLORIST

Teleflorist is the brand name of British Teleflower Service Ltd, one of the world's leading gift delivery companies. Every year, florists in the Teleflorist network deliver millions of bouquets throughout the British Isles and in 140 other countries worldwide.

For more information about Teleflorist, you can visit the company's website at www.teleflorist.co.uk, or simply call in to any florist where you see the distinctive dove logo.